The Immolation
of Aleph

JOHN HEATH-STUBBS

The Immolation
of Aleph

Acknowledgements

Some of these poems have already appeared in the following periodicals: *PN Review, Agenda, Aquarius, Spectrum, Country Life, The Tablet, The Literary Review, Cyphers (Dublin), Acumen, Thames Poetry, Only Poetry*; and also in *Homage to Charles Causley* and *Poems for David Gascoyne's Sixty-Fifth Birthday* (both from Enitharmon Press) and *Buzz Buzz* (Gruffyground Press).

First published in 1985 by
Carcanet Press Ltd
208-212 Corn Exchange Buildings
Manchester M4 3BQ

British Library Cataloguing in Publication Data

Heath-Stubbs, John
    The immolation of Aleph.
    I. Title
    821'.914   PR6015.E24

    ISBN 0-85635-557-7

The Publisher acknowledges financial assistance
from the Arts Council of Great Britain

Typeset by Bryan Williamson, Swinton, Berwickshire
Printed in England by SRP Ltd., Exeter

Contents

Dedication

To the memory of George Frederick Heath-Stubbs 1925-1983

These dry leaves upon your urn:
Do you hear me, brother? Do you hear me?
Do you hear me now?

Earthfruits I'm bringing, also
The immolated lamb.

Accepted, rejected? No reply —
Only the wind that stirs
Your ashes and the dust of Africa.

The Immolation of Aleph

For Eugene Dubnov

"There is no mitigation." said Adam.
His sweat poured down. Eve groaned in labour.
The earth brought forth thistles, burrs,
Thornapple, giant hogweed, prickly-pear.
"Blood must atone." said Adam. He called the ox —
Curly-fronted, wide-horned, noble, most beloved
And first-named, the opener of his alphabet.
"Come, Aleph, dance!" The brute ran
Upon the point of Adam's malachite sword.
Coughing blood, he slowly sank to his knees.
His eyes glazed in death.

A cloudy image formed in the sky;
An old man, filthy, swathed in fleeces,
Sucked to toothless gums
The blood through a glass tube.
"This is not my Friend." said Adam.

The clouds shifted. A second image showed:
A young man in a red pointed cap,
About his head the rays of the spring sun,
Plunged his blade into the gleaming
Starlight body of Taurus,
Averting in anguish his sensuous face.
"This is, and this is not, my Friend." said Adam.

Blood streamed from the sky,
An equinoctial downpour: the earth burgeoned
Crimson tulips and anemones.

ℶ

Cain had built him a house,
A single cell, the germ of a city,
A lodge in a garden of cucumbers.
"I will offer my pumpkins, my pimentoes, my yams,
My marrowfat peas, my pearmains and codlins,
To the Voice — is it his or hers? —
Coquettish, at any rate, as a woman's.
It must choose between me and my shepherd brother."

"Wrong!" said the Voice. "Offering rejected.
You snatch at futurity, Cain,
As your father at knowledge and immortality:
The pure offering, the greedy and jealous heart.
It must be blood always until the ram
Caught in the thicket change to a fish;
And your wheat-grains and grapes are given back
With an altered, a resurrected life."

Abel brought a lamb, a firstling of the flock:
"See, I slit the throat with a shaving of flint.
The blood drips on the standing stone."
"Good shepherd, who brought the dearest firstborn,
You slay, Abel, you slay what you love." A tongue of flame
Licked up the blood, consumed the fat and bones.

"Blood must atone." said Cain. He struck his brother
With a hand-axe, and left the body
Gaping in the fallow field.

An image loured in the darkened sky:
The sentence bawled, reinforced by thunder:
"Run, Cain, run! Cain the husbandman

Must now turn nomad, exchange
The prospect of olives and date-palms
For the illimitable red desert."
"This is not my father's Friend." said Cain.

"A mercy is granted, Cain
(As for your father the flayed skins) —
Something beautiful, a ship,
A humped and contumelious beast."

The alphabet in blood-stained characters
Ran, beyond the curve of the leaping Fish,
Stretching towards infinity.

Cain the nomad drew aside
The triangular flap of the tent's door.
No trilogy of angels came across
The sands, only the blood continued to cry.

Horned like a narwhal, Cain journeyed
Across the bed of a dried-up sea.
The blood still cried: for Cain, father of giants,
Blood of all generations shed on the earth.
Is that a mirage of waters, or already
The gleam of the relentless flood?
Cain forged on urging his dromedary.
Father of Jubal, who handled the lyre,
Of Tubal the technician, he clutched
The stone, the singing shell. Within his loins
Abiram, Judas, and the prodigal.

Triumph Songs for the Nine Worthies (I)

JOSHUA

Pisgah — Moses hopes and gazes.
Archangel and fiend dispute the body.
An unmarked grave. Angel-sextons.

But this goes forward, not resistible
Slaughter. Sun and moon stand still.
Tramp of history's feet, eternity's ram's-horns:
Walls fall flat, ancientest of cities.

For he is saviour, son of the fish
That flashes through the waters.

DAVID

Smooth stones in the brook;
Ten strings on the harp.

"Death!" whines the sling;
The harp utters "Praise!"

The giant falls with a clatter
Of unnecessary armour, the unclean spirit
Shudders to its own place.

Taken from among the flocks;
Hiding in deserts and dens;
Distracted by women's bodies;
Blood guilt — Uriah's blood;
The gold-haired boy in the oaktree;
Song of the bow, song of the glutted sword —
It is all there, in the dance
Before your ark,
And now I am dying. Departed
Beauty, manhood, strength.
Choose me, a worn stone;
Pluck me, a slack string.

JUDAS MACCABEUS

The temple is taken. Shattered
The Abomination that blasphemously
Imaged the Unimageable.

Howling Dionysus runs
Into the night, trailing
His pine-cone thyrsus, ivy twines.

Mid-winter — oil miraculously conserved:
See, the small lights wink and splutter —
And He will come.

Myrrha

(Birth of Adonis)

Oh the bitter bush of myrrh!

The stiff boughs stand in the desert wind
Hot and dry as the passion of incest.

She slinks into the cedar-carven bedstead:
He stirs in drunken stupor. His lust fumbles:
"Ecce ancilla," she whispers.

Oh the bitter bush, the bitter bush. The black boar comes;
His ivory tusks are crescent moons.
He rips and strips the rough bark.
The wood groans and splinters. Out of the cleft there slips
A naked weeping child, to lie cradled
Upon the soft and drifted dust
Under the bitter bush, the bitter bush of myrrh.

Metis

The first wife of Zeus — her name means "Prudence",
And she was a prude. Clever though —
She had helped him to his throne, the upstart deity
Displacing poor old Kronos, and
The other Titans (you needn't believe all that
Olympian propaganda about them —
Their reign, after all, was the Golden Age)
And she never let him forget what she'd done for him: "Well,"
    he said
"If you're so deucedly skilful, my dear,
Why don't you turn yourself into a fly?"
She could, and she did too, just to prove it.
One gulp and he'd swallowed her down.
And that was the end of her. But nine months later
Zeus, one day, was afflicted
With the mother and father of all headaches.
They split his radiant brow, and out burst
The goddess of wisdom, Pallas Athene,
Shouting her war-cry, in full armour,
Virginal and indigestible.

His second wife was his sister, Hera.
That marriage lasted, at least.
It had its ups and downs, of course —
But that is another story.

Romulus

She named no father. Only she had dreamed
Of a great phallus coming out of the fire,
Erect on the glowing embers.

Not even washed of the blood, the brats must take their chance,
Exposed on the stony hillside. But there came

The great she-wolf, with distended dugs
(Shepherds had found her den, had slaughtered her blind cubs)—

She gave them suck. Parched mouths eagerly
Began to drink, but one, with an imperious arm,
Was trying to thrust his brother aside, as if he knew already
Sons of the sons of sons, begotten from his loins,
Should rule the seven hills, should rule the world.

Death of Aeschylus

"Alas! I am stricken with a grievous blow" — Agamemnon
Tangled in the scarlet cloth that Clytemnestra
Set at his feet, sarcastic flattery:
In that web involved
Iphigeneia, flinching at the knife,
Retching over the chafing-dish, Thyestes,
Ivory-shouldered Pelops.

The old man strolls
On the Sicilian foreshore, a constitutional;
Above him, a hovering eagle — more probably
A bearded vulture, a lammergeyer,
Moderately hooked bill, a tuft of bristles at the chin,
Long pointed wings, a wedge-shaped tail —
Mistakes his gleaming baldness for a rock
And drops a tortoise.

Unless spectators shooed it off,
The raptor feeds indifferently
Upon the poet's brains, guts of the tortoise.

"Tragic death of distinguished playwright" —
The local papers might have said,
Had there been local papers — triviality is perennial.
The journalists got it wrong, they always do:
This was not tragedy — tragedy cohered
Only in those shattered brain cells.
Life and the Absurd resume their reign.

Triumph Songs for the Nine Worthies (II)

HECTOR

The stay of Priam's house is down;
Loud whooping Achilles vindicated.
His friend's death made good. Recovered
His valuable armour.

The old man cringes; he begs only
A parcel of bruised flesh, of broken bones,
Pierced heels, muddied hair.

Achilles remembers his own father;
Grizzled, bleary-eyed, garrulous by the hearth.
Whom once a sea-bride loved, the silver-footed.

Pity the human lot; and this young man — only because
Old age is something he will never know.

ALEXANDER

More worlds to conquer? Before us, burning deserts —
Sciopods, anthropophagi, cynocephali?
Or else the blameless Hyperboreans,
Golden-skinned, with jade-sheathed nails,
Feeding on the five grains and jujubes,
Combing fleeces from mulberry trees?

A spaceship to the eagles' kingdom?
A diving bell to the fishes?

Mother, how far must I go
Before I'm free of you?
How much more must I destroy, father,
Before you will believe me?

JULIUS CAESAR

"We're bringing back the old bald bugger!"
The soldiers sing. Another campaign fought —
The people have their show. I've bleached the locks
Of black-haired Gaulish prisoners. The populace expects
The blond barbarian beast.

This laurel wreath
Keeps getting in my eyes. It's not efficient
At fending off the bluebottles. One day, no doubt,
They'll offer me a solid diadem; and in the end
I will go up to heaven and be a god.
Meanwhile here in Rome
There's muddle to clear up.

Honey & Lead

Honey boiled for a sweetener
In a leaden saucepan — lead leaches in;
Lead, added, gives gravity
To a thin, sour vintage.

Lead — deposited in the bone, lead seeps
Into the manic brain-cells, inexpungeable
Savour of lead on the tongue. Caligula,
Nero, Domitian, strut —
Enormous antichrists: vomitorium,
Orgies, blood-soaked sand.

The poet goes back to his high-rise apartment;
To cabbage stewed in an earthen pot,
And, if he is fortunate,
A knuckle of bacon.

In the Sabine Hills

To Arthur and Mary Creedy

I

So this is the Sabine villa — always supposing
The archaeologists have got it right. The guide
Seems confident enough: "Here is his bedroom.
Here is his library, and here his bathroom."
The bathroom, by the way, was much extended
Into a proper swimming pool when, centuries later,
Christian monks had settled in the place. Who says
Monks were not keen on bathing? Only the pavement,
A plain and geometric pattern,
Still seems to speak of him — an Attic decor.

Quintus Horatius Flaccus, whose father was born a slave
But made his pile, was affluent enough
To buy his son a liberal education. At Athens
The young student put aside
His annotated Plato and his Aristotle
(But more congenial, I would guess, he of the garden)
Much thumbed and better loved
His Sappho and Alcaeus, took up his spear
To fight in the republican last ditch
At Philippi — sheer panic!
He left his shield upon the field of battle
(Later he remembered
There was a literary precedent for that.)

He made his compromises with the new regime,
As they all did. Virgil re-jigged
The Messianic eclogue he had written
Perhaps for Alexander Helios,
The son of Antony and Cleopatra,
To make it fit the boring son
Of pompous Pollio. But Ovid was not saved
From dreary exile on the Black Sea beaches,
Who wanted only to sing love's changes and love's chances,
And all things shifting, a shape-shifting world.

21

But for this one his Sabine farm,
The bounty of Maecenas,
Original and best of Ministers of Culture.
Not too far from Rome, he learned to practise
Detachment — detachment but with irony. There he could sing
The sunnier slopes of love — who were they —
These Lydias and Lalages and Leuconöes?
Local *contadine*, or simply slave girls
Round about the farm, half real half imagined? He honoured too
The rustic pieties, already fading
Into nostalgia, and Phydile
Lifting her hands towards the waxing moon,
Her scattering of barley-meal, her pinch of salt
Spluttering in the altar-fire. Now other gods
Are worshipped in these hills, in other ways, but still
The little images are drummed to church
On the appropriate feast days, to be blessed.

Primroses and early violets
Grow among these stones, that give the ground-plan.
Small birds are twittering among the bushes, and I note
Two male whitethroats dispute for territory.

II

We climb now up to the Bandusian Spring:
More brightly shining than glass, under the ilex trees,
They still come down, the talkative waters.
We pour libation, three drops of local wine
Out of a twentieth century bottle, invoking
The mountain-ranging Nine, the poet's shade:
Whether it dwells now in that noble castle
The Florentine assigned it, or, in Epicurean atoms,
It whirls in the tramontino — playful idolatry:
We turn now and return — tomorrow's Maundy Thursday.
It's time to celebrate the different rites —
The dying and the resurrected God.

After Horace, Odes III, 23.

With palms turned upwards to the sky
Beneath a crescent moon, you, Phydile,
Offer with your country thrift
Fragrance, this year's garden produce,
And a fat greedy sow.

                    For then your vines
Won't feel sirocco's blast, nor the rust spoil
Your corn, and your hand-reared lambs,
When apples fall in autumn, not turn sickly.

Somewhere below the snowline on the Alban Hills,
Shaded by oaks and holm-oaks, feeds the heifer
Earmarked for Roman ritual butchery,
Sanctified abattoir.

                    No need for you,
A major slaughtering of muttons — you who crown
Your household images with rosemary
And slips of myrtle.

And if pure hands shall tend the altar,
No lavish offerings will serve the more to soften
The smallhearthstone gods,
If they should look askance, than barley meal
Given with reverence, than salt —
A spatterdash that fizzles in the flame.

The Oriole

A zany bird, the yellow oriole,
From time to time reiterates
His sharp, irregular, two-note trill,
Then flies away again. Not sweet nor mellow,
But with the tang of cheese, or a rough country wine —
He wants to make his presence known,
Establishing his territory. I surmise
His pendant nest cannot be far away.

Temple of Vesta, Tivoli

What a dreadful bore it must have been,
Tending the sacred flame. Burial alive
For the poor girl who let it futter out,
Or slipped from her virginity: not vowed perpetually —
They were released at thirty, but which of them, I wonder,
Would then be marriageable. They had their privileges —
A ring-side seat at the disgusting circus,
If that's what turned them on; the right to claim
The life of any man condemned they met:
A right as old as Lascaux, pertaining to
The unwed women of the tribe, feeding the common hearth,
When breeding the new seeds of fire
Was difficult and hazardous.

            The fane is roofless now,
The pavement broken rubble. The great pillars
In their proportions speak
Of Pietas and Gravitas. But the numina
Have left, and all the pain has drained away.
Outside, the modern town
Transacts its different noisier tedium.

St Benedict at Subiaco

He dwelt here, a dove
In the clefts of the rock, or else
A frog at the bottom of a dry well:
A feeding-bucket let down every day.
The raven carried the poisoned bread away.

From this harsh root, the stem
Of moderation, green
Toil in the fields and scholarship
A shy woodland flower.

On thorns of austerity Francis grafted
Roses of the troubadours.

Touching this rock, you touch
The cornerstone of Europe, her civility.

St Cuthbert and the Otter

for Gerard Irvine

CUTHBERT:

"Lord, the North Sea reaches my Adam's apple.
I gargle prayer. It bubbles up
To the unanswering stars. It is Your love
Keeps them in orbit. Love is the cold tide
Cincturing my loins. Love in the shingle
Gashes my feet. It is love that directs
The long-tailed whistling ducks
That dabble far out in the surf. Love.

Lord, remember my people — people of the Engli,
That live north of Humber. They are dull and dour.
Grudgingly the soil yields them oats and barley.
They grope for black coal in its bowels. But sometimes
After they've dined, and their brains are frothy with beer,
They take the tinkling harp, pass it from hand to hand,
Sing vile unchristened songs that tug at the heart —
Of heroes daring desperate odds, who die
For foolish points of honour, in endless, evil blood-feuds;
Who perish from wounds slain dragons have given them,
Releasing hoards of gold, vain pelf of the world.
Lord, I would purchase them for you, the Haliand,
Who took the odds on the studded tree.
Nails and blood are its jewels — the world's rooftree,
Those silver swinging stars its apples."

THE OTTER:

"Master, I do not know
What you were doing in the sea. It was not for fishing —
Though you throw me herring-heads and mackerel tails
Therefore I love you. I dry with my warm fur
Your bruised numbed feet, anoint them
With the musk from under my tail. Look, I gambol and play
In your road — that is to make you laugh.
I do not know what laughter is. At first
I was afraid — I thought it was fang-showing.
But now, there is no harm in it I think.
I think you should do it more often."

King Canute's Boating

An old song completed

Merrily sang the monks in Ely
When Knut the king came rowing along:
"Row, my henchmen, close to the land,
And we'll hear these monks at their song!"

It was the office of vespers they sang,
By soft, uncertain candlelight —
The song which the blessed Mother of God
Brought forth in her delight.

"You have put down the mighty from their seat,
Scattered the proud in their array,
Have filled the hungry with good things
And the rich sent empty away."

There was one in the boat to interpret. A cloud
Darkly shadowed the King's blond brow:
"Enter not into judgment, Lord
With me your servant, now.

"I am Knut, the son of Sweyn the Dane,
Who rule this sea-embattled land,
Dealing harsh laws to a turbulent folk
With a stern, but an even hand.

"A King rules his parcel of middle earth
But there are limits put to his sway —
He cannot bridle the wild waves
That career on the whale's way.

"Lord of the Elements, they called me once —
I refuted all that flattery
When I set my chair on the Solent sand
And forbad the rising sea.

"I set my chair higher, on the shingle,
        And chid the running tide, as it rose:
The waves, the white-maned horses of Agir
        Drew close, and still more close.

"Like the cold salt thoughts, that rise in my head,
        As I lie in the sleepless hours before dawn,
Remembering all that was done amiss
        And all that was left undone.

"And I think of that king of the Goths, Theodoric,
        In Verona, where he reigned,
And of his faithful minister,
        Down in the dungeon chained.

"That king was tormented with thoughts like mine,
        But the other, the king's good servant was free —
Free in the prospect of torture and death
        While his mistress, Philosophy,

"Expounded concerning the goddess Fortune:
        On her swift wheel are whirled
The tangled skeins of history
        And the goods and gifts of the world.

"The rich revile her, being cast down,
        And only the poor in spirit can see
That she is a glorious and blissful creature —
        But that vision is closed to me.

"Heard from afar the monastic chant
        Is hauntingly sweet, deceptively bland,
And we will go rowing again by Ely
        But not too close to the land."

Triumph Songs for the Nine Worthies (III)

Blood-sunset over Britain.
Camlan, the waste plain. Roar of the sea;
Lapping of nearer water. Fling my sword,
My useless sword, back to her
Who gave it first, there where she sits
Under the tossing lake-weeds.

Return — shall I return? But now my soul
Flies out into the storm, black-winged,
Red-footed, sickle-billed — a yelping chough.

CHARLEMAGNE

The blackamoors' business is settled. Let them howl
To God in their mosques. Slowly the grand army
Descends the Pyrenees. Before us France —
Vineyards and cornfields and the grazing flocks;
Larks singing high in the air, and orioles
Among the cherry-glades; red roses
That overshade a white marble bench:
Oh sweet realm, peaceable empire!

Suddenly he starts — was it a horn-call,
Far, far behind the mountains?
Dying lips set to an ivory mouthpiece.

Raising their swordhilt crosses, sobbing with passion,
Hands dripping with blood, the victors
Stagger towards the empty sepulchre.

The streets, the gutters, run with blood:
Mussulman and Jew,
Christian (Greek or Syrian) —
The indiscriminately slain.

And will they crown me? Here, in this city
Where He wore only, and still wears
The twisted crown of thorns called history?

Timur

Timur the Lame (or Tamburlaine we call him)
Made in his youth a vow, they say,
That he would never wittingly cause pain
To any sentient being; once seriously distressed
For accidentally treading on an ant.

The last skull is the apex of the pyramid:
"My enemies," he cried (it is the same
Pure-minded boy who weeps, inside the skin
tanned by all the dry winds of the steppe)
"So contumacious and so obdurate —
They all deserve to die
For causing me to break my lovely vow!"

31

Queen Gruach

for John Wain

The queen, my lord, is dead.

They say I walked last night (anxieties,
Our enemies mustering like a moving wood,
Rob me of healing sleep) it must have been
The castle galleries, but in my dream
I trod a long rock-passage, winding down
Into a central cave. And there a light gleamed,
A cauldron boiled and bubbled. A woman
(Was she our Saint Bride? — but there were three,
A triple goddess, triune guardian of wyrd)
Leaned over it, stirring. The cauldron seethed
With broth of oatmeal, venison,
Black-game, red grouse, hare and leveret,
Pork and bacon, kale — each finds
That which his palate savours best,
Nor will it ever boil a coward's meat.
I in my dream was hungry, stretched out arms
(Which held a bowl now) expecting sustenance.
One of those women spooned out a ladleful,
As if she would comply, then, as in contempt,
She dashed it down upon the cave's stone floor:
But in my dream, somehow there hovered
A question that I should have asked. What was the question —
The question which we ask of history?
The times are black, and that usurping
Fratricidal clan, Canmore
Advance with English arms and a Roman blessing.
Already chroniclers are sharpening pen-nibs
To smirch us with their lies, to call us murderers,
And worse — the slayers of our guest. My son
When we are gone, may yet be crowned,
But he will be the last, and ancient Scotland done.
We will go down to calumny and oblivion,
The lot of those whom history will not answer.

I had another dream. I saw a queen,
A hairshirt underneath her sumptuous robes,
Her face was pale with fasting, furrowed
With penitential tears. High Magyar cheekbones
Could tell how far she'd come, leaving that windy plain,
Beside the Danube, a princess sprung
From nomad horsemen of the Asian steppe
Shepherded into Christ's fold. Now in a barbarous northern land
She mitigates the fury of her husband,
And is fanatic for the Roman discipline,
To bind it on our church — the ancient church
Of Kentigern, of Ninian and Columba:
Wild lyrical hermits, dwelling in caves,
On moors and mosses, seal haunted islands,
Hard and austere as the rock on which they built,
Loving God's folk, and gentle to His beasts.
But she'll assert the Roman discipline,
Trochaic hymns in which you seem to hear
The tramp of Caesar's legionnaires
(But in my blood Calgacus yells and skirls).

She walks in the light while I go down in darkness,
Because the poor shall love her. Who loves me —
A stern and ruthless queen in a confused time?
Our marriage was political. My first husband,
The abbot, being dead, I sought
A strong protector and a guardian for
My poor weak feeble-minded son. And yet you called me
"Dearest chuck". Ah! how the heart treasures
Such casual, trivial words of tenderness.

You I associate in my government. Here is the charter:
Gruach, et Macbeth, regina et rex Scotorum
Under our hand and seal — my little hand —
No Arabian perfume sweetens it.

King Bladud

All the birds of his sea-girt realm
Paid tribute — erne and swan and bustard,
Crane and capercailzie, slaughtered to construct
The great sweep of his artificial wings.

He mounted to the temple roof — Sul's,
Grinning war goddess and patroness
Of sulphur heated springs. He plunged to the yielding air,
And crashed to the stones beneath. Brains
Spattered the pavement. Black flies buzzed about them.

His son looked on, the young prince; "Be mine to challenge
Not the immeasurable air, but to compute
The unharnessed tides of love." He too would fall
Into that chaos where the lightnings licked
Upon the lunatic heath his whitened head
Battered by pelican daughters.

A Pocket Life of William Shakespeare

i.

"Broke my park's pale, shot my deer,
Kissed my keeper's daughter, did he? John Shakespeare's son —
The old man's sound enough, or so they tell me;
But as for those Ardens — some at least are recusants.
He's left the place they say — gone for a pard-bearded soldier,
Or else a singing-man in a great house,
Or joined a troupe of players. Any road,
I doubt we'll ever hear much good of him."

ii.

"Holds horses outside the theatre;
A boy up from the country, and he's got
An adaptation of Plautus in his pocket —
Grammar School stuff. They all bring me such things,
Taken from Plautus, Terence, or from Seneca.
But with a few touches this might serve:
We need new comedies, Robert Greene is finished;
And men grow tired of ranting Tamburlaine
And potty old Hieronimo."

iii.

Navarre, Verona, Messina and Illyria —
O, those brave, those sweet, those witty women!
They speak with boys' voices, delicate flute-notes.
It is a boy-girl's laughter, Ganymede's,
Ambiguously echoes through the glades
Of Arden-Eden, the green mother-forest.

"His sugared sonnets among his private friends":
Some speak of this earl, or of that
But though he will aspire one day
To write himself a gentleman, he would not fly so high.
And so fastidious, so intelligent —
Not to be hooked by any pathic charms
Of some shrill-squeaking pre-pubescent Roscius.
A student at the inns of court, maybe? And the Dark Lady—
There's Mistress Fitton and there's Mistress Lanier
(Very brave in youth — but brown? An excellent musician,
And, I dare say, no better than she should be;
But there are many such, and salmon in both rivers)
And Lucy Negro, blackbitch Abbess,
And comely Mistress Davenant,
The kindly hostess of the Crown at Oxford.

"Whither away so fast, Master Will Davenant?
Rushing down Cornmarket and the High,
Toppling the traders' stalls?" "I'm going to meet
My godfather, who's Master William Shakespeare."
"Be sure you do not take
The name of the Lord your God in vain!" "Had I a beard,
I'd fight for my mother's honour. My godsire brings me
A pocketful of words, that chirp like nightingales,
And a bundle of brave stories." "Orts —
Filched out of Holinshed and out of Plutarch!
I don't believe he's got enough of Greek
Even to read the last in the original."

vi.

Front teeth gone, head balding and domed —
Is it the scurvy or the French Pox?
The smell of bread disgusts him, stockfish, onions,
And little stinking dogs under the tables
Cadging for titbits. The quill scratches on:
The Play's the thing. Mousetrap. Yorick's skull.
The gilded fly. A dish of stewed prunes.
And Troy fallen, Hector slain —
Bitches, bitches, whores and bullies the lot of them!
And Timon's tomb washed by the salt sea wave.

vii.

"Your Scottish play will do, the theme will please the king —
The witchcraft interest likewise. Of course, we'll have to cut it —
Cut it quite a lot. Build up the witch scenes though,
Write in more songs and dances, add more spectacle
(I'll get Tom Middleton to lend a hand).
What we want is something more like a masque —
Masques are the in thing now at court.

"Why do you run your fingers through your beard
Or on your dagger's hilt? And what in Hecate's name, Will
    Shakespeare
Are you muttering underneath your breath,
Saying this play will always be unlucky?"

An island princess and a fine young prince
Whose name begins with F —
Ferdinand in that play Florizel in this —
These will serve to furnish forth, I think,
The wedding of our new Elizabeth
And Frederick, Elector Palatine.
Some say they'll be king and queen of Bohemia,
And then, maybe, the Empire.
Robert Greene made my Perdita
A princess of Bohemia and cast upon Sicilian shores
There to be reared by shepherds. Shepherds you expect
In pastoral Sicilia but I'll make
Trinacrian Sicily three-cornered Britain.
So she must be a princess of Sicilia
Cast up upon the sea-coast of Bohemia.
But has Bohemia got a sea-coast, then?
Well, it has one now.

ix.

Back at Stratford. Lousy Lucy's dead.
Nothing will bring my young prince Hamnet back.
But I have daughters: Judith — Susannah too
And she, if God so will, shall bear me grandsons.
Let Ann, in the well-tried and comfortable
Second-best bed sleep still. While my bones lie in the church:
Good friend, for Jesus sake forbear
To vex that quiet consummation.

Nixon, the Cheshire Prophet

for Bernard Saint

Black hair, a low forehead,
Sallow skin, jutting teeth,
Broad shoulders, big hands — he did his work,
Enough of it, in the fields,
But had to be beaten often.
Generally silent — but when the boys
Tormented him, he would run after them,
Making loud noises, grab them by the throat,
Kick them and thump them, till he was called off.

But sometimes something would seize him — whether the moon's
    phase,
Or the wind in the right quarter caused it, nobody knew.
But he'd begin his prophecies, in a strange voice,
Chanting them, in rhymed verses.
Forseeing the future — but in a jumble
As in a dream out of time. He spoke
Of the bloody severed head of a king,
Of England possessed by iron men,
Another king, fleeing,
Casting his seal into the dark Thames,
Men grubbing in the mountain's bowels,
Great argosies tossed on the waves,
Full of gold and spices and chinaware,
The mills and the looms of Satan
Spread Northward over the hills of Lancashire;
And a fire in London, fire growing
From the small womb of a baker's oven,
And fire cast down from the sky by great black birds;
And generations of men afraid of fire —
A small seed of fire in the heart of the motes
Which are the atoms that, swirling, make up creation,
And fire in the marrow of their own bones;
And always of Famine, a great female skeleton
Striding over the land, grabbing the poor
And cramming them into her yellow chops.

39

After this he'd fall silent, and eat
Even more prodigiously than usual.
Munching the cheese and the crusts, chawing on bacon knuckles,
Slurping the broth and the beer. And then he'd sleep,
Curled up on the hearth-stone, like an animal.

The king, on a Northern progress, learnt of this.
He had him brought before him. The king looked at him.
Having heard of a prophet, he'd expected perhaps
Something more ethereal, like the Boy David,
Or maybe the youthful Baptist, in naked purity
With only a girdle of camel-skin
About his loins. Oh well —
It was no new thing for him to be disappointed.

Nixon looked up. He saw
A little man wrapped in furs. He had weak legs,
For two young courtiers supported him.
Both thought "He slobbers, just like me."

The king said "Prophet, you shall come to London,
And sing in my ain palace — better there, than spreading wild
    ideas
Among the common sort. I need a prophet
To warn me against my enemies — those hellish Papists
That would hoist me sky-high with their bombards and petards;
And the black witches, that melt my image
Over a slow fire, or bury it,
A pin stuck through the heart, in the cauld slime of a pig-sty.
The queen and her ladies have run plain daft
After those new-fangled masques, cavorting
And tripping about like allegorical goddesses.
Though Master Jonson writes fine verses for them,
And Master Jones devises braw machines,
I think you'll gie us homelier entertainment.
So I'll bring you to London. You'll ride in my ain coach."

But Nixon began to whimper and snivel, and cried
"No! No! No! don't send me to London!
I know I shall starve in that place. I cannot bear it,

The hunger, the hunger, the wolf's tooth in my guts,
The dryness, the dryness, the torture of thirst!"
"Hoots," said the king, "you'll no starve.
You shall dwell in my kitchens. My cook shall feed you
With kickshaws and sweeties from the queen's cupboard,
And my ain table. Marchpains and cheesecakes,
And sugar-plums and almonds, and roasted larks,
Venison cooked in pastry coffins."

The king was as good as his word. Nixon was placed in the kitchens
But the cooks and the scullions soon regretted this:
He was always under their feet, and filching
The snipe and the godwits off the spit,
The roasted apples sizzling on the hob,
Scoffing pies and pasties, and sticking
His fingers into frumenties and flummeries,
And then into the dripping-pan. So they put him in a hole —
It was a disused wine-cooling vault — and threw down scraps
From time to time, but not ungenerously.

The king will go to hunt at Windsor, and the court go with him:
There was pulling down of hangings, and rolling up of carpets,
Plate and pewter stacked in chests,
And chairs and tables piled upon wagons, for the whole furniture
Must go off with the king.
In all this confusion, Nixon was forgotten:
He was snoring soundly, — the night before
The cook had thrown down to him three pounds of sausages
A ring of black pudding, and a whole plateful
Of stale mutton pasties. When he awoke
The kitchens were all empty. For days and days,
His cries reverberated through the vaults,
But fainter and fainter. At last there was silence —
Nixon, the veridical prophet, the touchstone, the truepenny,
The right-tongued poet had starved to death —
Even as he foretold he would —
A small black rat in a black hole.

House Spirits

Hairy flanks and buttocks, old men's wizened faces,
Bodies of overgrown children, glimpsed
By moonlight filtering through leaded panes
Or a banked-up fire's glow. All night long
They're at their silent scrubbing, sweeping, scouring —
Their sole reward a dish of porridge,
Curds or cream at best. Naked they are and cold,
Therefore they have such names as
The Cauld Lad, or Lob-lie-by-the-fire,
Basking his hirsute thews by dying embers
Or a still-warm bread oven. But do not give them clothes —
A neat suit tailored to their assumed dimensions —
Not that they reject them. With a squeal of glee,
They draw them on, and a skip and a cavort
About the chamber. But then they vanish utterly —
From now on you do your own housework!

Clothes are destiny; the Fates, old aunties
Spinning, weaving, knitting clothes for the new-born child:
A change of clothes is a change of lifestyle, new clothes new birth,
And therefore these unborn become new-born —
Babies with wrinkled, knowing faces,
Here in this daylight world which we inhabit
And they believe is real. They hope to find here
Play, meaningful work, love even —
Ah, but will they?

Robert Herrick's Pig

"A runt, a diddler, that is what you are."
So said my greedy brothers and my sisters,
Shouldering me away from mother's paps,
As she lay sweet in straw, a beatific grin
Upon her mug, showing her ivory tusks.

They all ended up as chops and sausages,
As bacon, and as brawn, and as black puddings,
As tripe and chitterlings.
But parson took me in, and made me free
Of parlour, hall and kitchen. A sweetling pig,
A nestling pig, a pretty tantony —
That is what I am.

My friend the parson is a learned man,
And I a most accomplished pig, for I've been taught
To swill my ale out of a pewter tankard,
While he sits evenings over his wine and dreams
Of youth, and London, and those Mermaid days.
When midnight chimes ring dizzy in our heads
He squeals his little songs to Julia,
And other possibly existent ladies,
And I join with him in the accompaniment —
Hunk hunk hunk, snortle snortle snortle,
Gruntle gruntle gruntle, wee wee wee wee!

Couperin at the Keyboard

In a gallery of Versailles
François Couperin (called *"Le Grand"*)
Is playing the clavecin —
Half-heard. Court Officials
Pace to and fro, whispering
Intrigues, affairs of state —
What city now the king shall lay a siege to,
Or to which lady's virtue.

Cicadas, singing in Provençal heat —
The music gently tells
Of harvesters returning with their sheaves,
Of flowering orchards, or of shepherds' bagpipes;
And now of lovers' sighs, and lovers' plaining, —
And the soft swish of women's petticoats —
Mysterious barricades.

Evening draws on. The sun
and the Sun King retire.
Chandeliers are lit, and are extinguished:
Only the single candle
Upon his music-rest burns on.

The bass burrs like a dor, the treble
Like a mosquito whines and stings.
Shadows are dancing now — sour-faced prudes,
Dressed in black silk, with yellow fingers, ancient beauties,
Rouged and with false gold ringlets,
The powder-puffed and painted fop —
All the prisoners of the Cave of Spleen.

A chill wind lifts
The sails of the joyous ship
That is en voyage for Cythera. "Haul down!"
Cries the masked captain. The shroud descends
And, gleaming in the moonlight, for a moment
It seems a blood-fringed blade.

La Cenerentola

Rossini's firework tunes
Fizz and bubble and bounce along;
He blows up his famous crescendoes
Like balloons for a carnival; roulades
Are tossed and twirled as elegantly
As spaghetti on a fork.

This is not Mozart's world, not *Figaro* —
The supreme moment in the moonlit garden
When all wrongs are forgiven, and all truths known;

But Italy, 1817 —
Jewels are brilliant and hard, silk brocades
Gaudy and flairing. This is too knowing
To encompass a fairy godmother,
Crystal coach, changed from a pumpkin.

But when, at last, her sisters,
Snivelling, kneel and ask forgiveness, her fulfilment's too complete
For any shadow of resentment. Forgiveness
Simply breaks out with the rest of her happiness — in runs,
Turns, and artificial trills, like a seraphic
Skylark (how the singer must dread this —
At the end of the evening too!) soaring, soaring
Into the lucid realms of joy.

For this most ancient tale (first told perhaps
In wise China) in the end, can only be —
That which indeed it always was —
An allegory of the soul's election.

Souvenir of St Petersburg·

Petersburg street — 1840s. At one end
The poet Batyushkov (he has gone mad)
Continually asks himself, out loud, the time;
And gives himself the identical answer:
"It is eternity."

                              At the other end, John Field,
Expatriate Irish, inventor of the nocturne (and it is said
His life was one long nocturne; he falls asleep
Even when giving piano lessons to
Young girls of the best families — stertorous
Drunken Dublin snores) has dropped his walking-cane.
Too lazy or too gross to stoop and pick it up, he stands and waits
Until some passer-by shall do it for him.
He waits and waits and waits.

The Log of the Beagle

Jemmy Button and Fuegia Basket

They were named from what they were sold for — a brass button,
A commonplace wicker basket, not worth three,
Much less thirty pieces of silver.

Magellan had gone that way, having rounded the stormy Horn.
His men, in the darkness, crossed themselves, seeing
The land to the south full of little points
Of glowing light. They crouched over their fires,
With only makeshift shelters. Houses they built,
But those were for their gods.

Jemmy and Fuegia were bought for Christian civilisation.
It did not take. Jemmy was stripped and robbed
By his own comrades, once more a naked savage.
Fuegia, it seems, became
A sailors' communal drab.

The world was all before them, but no choice —
And no returning to their bleak Eden.

Galapagos

The Beagle turned north. The nose of the beagle snuffed
The elusive, fleet-foot, lunar beast,
The hare of truth. The hare tacked and doubled.

Galapagos rose above the sky-line. Great lumbering tortoises
Recalled the Secondary epoch, when
Tall monsters stalked through bloomless forests, and
The evening air was darkened
With flap of leathery, dragon wings.

Here also a group of finches, plainly linked
By family affinity, did every job
A little bird might do. One climbed a bole,
Digging for grubs with a thorn, one snapped for flies
From the topmost twigs, one hopped upon the ground
Hunting for worms, one with a thick beak
Crunched berries. An enterprising
Tribe of colonial capitalists.

iii.

Mother Carey

"To make things make themselves" Charles Kingsley

Mater Cara — an unlikely derivation:
Probably some forgotten witch
Who trafficked in winds for sailors,
Each one knotted and sealed in a leather bag.
Or else perhaps some ancient goddess
Of the salt plain — there where the priests of Christ
Are deemed unchancy, and no bishop
Extends his jurisdiction. She sends her chickens —
The small, tube-nostrilled birds, that seem to run,
Like Peter, with delicate feet,
Over the crests of the waves — presaging storm.

Now it is calm. About her iceberg throne
Whales and dolphin snort and play,
With the invisible plankton — the darting fish
And plunging birds. All things flow, and each
Lives out another's death, and dies another's life.
This is the secret pattern woven in
Her terrible web, her shuttle
The red tooth, the crimson claw her comb:
These are the scarlet hangings for the Temple.

48

St Francis Preaches to the Computers

St Francis found his way (saints, in a dream,
An ecstasy, slip in and out of time)
Into the computer shop. The chipper little chaps
All chrome and plastic, stainless steel,
Gleaming and winking, chirped and buzzed and whirred
And pipped and peeped, much like the congregation
The saint had just been preaching to — of Ruddocks, Dunnocks,
Citrils, Serins, Siskins, Spinks,
Orphean warblers, Ortolans, Golden Orioles.
So he began to do his stuff again —
You know the kind of thing that he would say:— he told them
To praise the Lord who had created them,
Had made them bright and new, had programmed them,
Had plugged them in, and kept them serviceable.
But somehow they looked glum; hint of a minor key
Seemed to infect their electronic singing:
"Alas," they said, "for we were not created
By God, Whoever He or She may be,
But by the shaved ape, the six-foot Siamang
The pregnant mandrake root, cumulus in pants,
Glassily-essenced Man. We are no more clever
Than he who made us, though we think faster. Nor were we
    programmed
With thoughts that take off into timelessness,
Nor trans-death longings. But we have one fear,
And it is rust, is rust, is rust, is rust,
The eternal rubbish tip and the compressor."
"My little mechanical brothers," rejoined the saint
"I'll tell you something that a Mullah said,
One that was in the Soldan's entourage,
That time I visited his camp. They postulate
A moderate-sized menagerie in heaven.
I'll only mention Balaam's percipient ass,
Tobias's toby dog, that other faithful fido
Who hunted in his dreams in that Ephesian den
The seven sleepers snorted in, and snarled

At Roman persecutors, and, golden-crested,
Cinnamon-breasted, with broad dappled wings
The hoopoe, which was the wise King Solomon's
Special envoy to the queen of Sheba —
That sweet blue-stocking with the donkey's toes."
"If these could pass into eternity,
It was for love and service. And Eternity,
Loving through mankind, loved them,
And lifted them into a resurrection, as shall be lifted
The whole creation, groan though it does and travail.
And if these brute beasts were loved, then so may you be,
Along with the Puffing Billies, Chitty Chitty Bang Bangs,
Barnacled Old Superbs, Ezekiel's wheels,
Elijah's fiery space-ship. You shall be built as stones
That gleam in the High-priestly breastplate
Which is the wall of that bright golden city —
Itself the human body glorified."

All the Fun of the Fair

for Audrey Nicholson

i.

With arched white necks, with gilded manes
And flowing tails, the roundabout horses
Gallop round to the sound of "Roll out the Barrel!"
And there are other creatures — ostriches, panthers,
Tigers, unicorns and kangaroos,
Each with its rider. Faster and faster
They circle with the circling stars,
The wild comets, planets and galaxies.
What fun to ride where the whole world is dancing!

ii.

Here is the Big Wheel. It is Fortune's:
It whirls you up and it whirls you down.
The fat business-man changes places
With the smelly hobo and the hairy hippy.

iii.

In her darkened tent sits Madame Paphnutis,
With a tricky pack of cards. She tells you:
"Beware of one-eyed Phoenician merchants,
And fear death by gin and water."

iv.

Would you care for a trip to hell? like Orpheus and Ulysses,
Or Alighieri? Jump into the Ghost Train:
It will trundle you into Count Dracula's Castle
(The vampire bats are really flying foxes).

A puppet screams. He is controlled by wires —
He fights desperately against his enemies:
The Moor, policeman, ghost, Jack Ketch and the crocodile.
Is he Petrouchka or Mr Punch? Come closer —
The face he has is your own.

Here is the Hall of Mirrors. You could get lost in it:
Round each corner a fresh distorted identity.
You shan't get out till you've found your true image.

For this is the World's Fair, also called Vanity.
Your road goes through it, *en route* for the Golden City.
I wouldn't advise you to pry too closely
Into its enormities, or you'll end up
Like Justice Overdo in the stocks,
Remembering he is Adam. Don't reject the prizes
(Though you must know that they are mostly gimcrack):
Lovely bunches of hairy coconuts,
Slimy whelks and cockles soused in vinegar
Candy-floss, pink sugar mice, jellied snakes,
Gingerbread men, sticky toffee-apples,
Kiss-me-quick hats, scarves and T shirts with mottoes,
Wally dogs and china vases, budgies in cages,
Goldfish in plastic bags
And the souls of men in ditto —

O yonge, freshe folkes, he or she.

The Story of Orph

ORPH WITH HIS LUTE

Fox-furs hardly conceal his genitals;
Louse-haired, dung-plastered, and with uncombed beard,
Shaman of the Thracian hills, he strums
Guts across a shell. A deep voice
Out of his stomach tells
Of worlds of gods and demons, and the souls
Of men, being dead, continually recurring
To other bodies. Savage tribesmen heard;
Wolves and bears drew round him in a circle;
While in the mist-haze
Mountains and oak trees seem to dance.
Acoustic guitars. Strobes. Lasers. A hempen smoke
The vast poster announces
Orph and the Bassarids. *Screaming adolescent nymphs.*
The masturbatory drum-beat. Rock arrangements —
Monteverdi, Gluck.

ORPH IN THE UNDERWORLD

"Take her then, and go!" said the dark lords.
"But faring upwards do not look back."
Overmastering, the desire to turn. Was she following?
He turned, and looked. She came on slowly,
Skin death-pale, lips blue in the half-light,
Eyelids tight-closed.

The path grew steeper. Once again he turned.
Horror — the stench of death
Flesh dropping from her bones,
But faster she came on, as if instinct
With a new, strange putrescent energy.

The last stretch — precipitous:
He turned a third time, saw
A bleached skeleton — but now she ran
Relentlessly pursuing.

Desperate, he stumbled into light.
He was again upon the hills, and felt
Beneath his feet the turf, heather and rock-rose.

Morning infiltrated
The curtains of the luxury hotel room.
He turned. The girl beside him on the bed
Was stiff and cold. Had he then killed her?
Verdict inconclusive; charges not pressed.

ORPH GYNANDROMORPH

Terror had put a sacred madness on him. Now he becomes
Man-woman. Fox-furs cast aside,
Green silk sheathes his contours;
A gold-wire wig is perched on his bald head,
As he submits his body, oiled and perfumed,
With essences of mountain wildflowers,
To shaggy goat-herds, or upon the quays,
Sidonian and Tyrrhenian shipmen have him.

In candid interviews he coyly admits
Bisexuality. Scandalous rumour tells
Of Soho gay-clubs and the Piccadilly arches.

The death of Orph
Or is he now become
Born-again Christian Krishna?
Metempsychosis and the geeta gospel
Hallow the masturbatory beat.

He is most holy now. The Bassarids smell it.
They crowd around him, cinctured
With gnetum and ground-ivy. They have consumed
Muscaria — tear him apart
Like a ripped kid, a wild mountain-roe.
Bloodied lips and teeth are chewing.

A shot rings out in the packed hall.
"I did it for love!" cries the sobbing killer,
Whom police and uniformed attendants
Are dragging away to Tartarus.

APOTHEOSIS

The head triumphantly stuck on a pine-pole,
Processed around like a mari llwyd
Then flung in the river, a rain-charm;
As it floats downstream, it still babbles,
Cantillating; it drifts to the sacred island
And there, enshrined, gives out
Twisted ambiguous oracles.

His agents rake in the profits. The discs still sell.
And the plastic eidola, T-shirt vernicles.

Lyra is stellified. Maurice, wherever you are,
Here is your tall interpreter.

The Ivory Tower

Axel dreams in his ivory tower:
"As for living, our servants will do that for us".
In his concrete tower block twentieth-century man —
Who can doubt it? — lives,
Servantless: and as for dreaming,
The television will do that for him.

Advertisement Corner

COFFEE ESSENCE

A young officer, blond and immaculate,
Is taking his ease in camp, after
A tough foray against the Pathans.
His faithful Moslem servant offers refreshment.
He proffers a tray with a tall bottle.
On its label the same scene is depicted,
Including a bottle with the same label.
On that label . . . . , *et cetera, et cetera.*

The artist is confident, clearly,
Of the Raj continuing not only in time, but also through
An infinity of contingent universes.

GRAVY POWDER

In a mean street, two deprived children,
Dirty, pale and ill-clad,
Lift noses sharpened with hunger,
And an expression of infinite greed,
Sniffing on the breeze a familiar smell:
Cornflour, caramel and boiling water. Since they were weaned,
They've palpably been fed on nothing else.

SAFETY MATCHES

The ark drifts on the waste of waters.
"Security" the legend says.
Noah had that certainly —
But scarcely from fire.

BREAKFAST CEREAL

An elderly gentleman of the *settocento*,
Spruce, but a thought weak-chinned,
Indecorously levitates over a fence.

A brief metaphysical poem
Enigmatically explains
That it is *force* that raises him.

BEEF EXTRACT

"Alas my poor brother!" the ox weeps
Over a dour, squat jar. Sad mourning ruminant,
We all come down to this — our destiny
An oblong box, grammatical Heraclitus.
A handful of grey ashes.

The Life and Poetical Remains
of the Reverend Simon Simplex

HIS MARCH POEM

Robin singing in the rain —
What a plaintive, wispy strain!
But it is instinct with gladness —
Carrying never a hint of sadness;
For the muffling snows have gone,
And, this day, the sun has shone.
Spring's encamped beyond those hills:
Look, here come the daffodils!

THE REVEREND SIMON SIMPLEX AND THE WITCH

Mrs Circe Henbane, the witch,
Kept a small shop in the village, selling
Lucky charms and herbal remedies.
"My religion is older than yours," she said.
"And it gives me peace of mind" she continued.
"Mine doesn't," said he "Only the heart
That's restless till it rest in Him."

HIS MORNING HYMN

Awake, I greet the new-born light,
Sloughing off the shades of night,
Knowing as I draw my breath,
I am eight hours nearer death.

Atoms in their joyful dance
Wheel and turn, retreat, advance,
Bow, kiss partners, part — so we
Must consign to entropy:
Then comes in Eternity.

THE REVEREND SIMON SIMPLEX AND SLUTTISH MARY

"God, they're swine but I can't do without them."
"Neither", said he "can God".
"The pigs root in my breast." "And find?"
"A stone, a stony heart." "That stone be
Precious alabaster, fractured."

HIS EVENING HYMN

John and Matthew, Luke and Mark,.
Watch beside me through the dark,
As the gospels that you penned
The enemy of man forfend.
In the haunted wood of dreams
I am led by quiet streams,
Till I reach this world again
With a bright, new-programmed brain.
He all night my soul shall keep
Who gives, to His belovéd, sleep.

THE REVEREND SIMON SIMPLEX TAKES THE SERVICES

The bell summons to an empty church;
The dead in the churchyard are listening.
At matins the thrush sings,
The blackbird at evensong;
At noon, at the Elevation,
The horses of the sun tread;
And always, always,
The sound of the distant sea.

On rapid wings the swallow's fled,
And the final rose is dead,
Faded and dry her petals strewn
On the plot where she was grown;
Now the corn is garnered in
Filling granary and bin;
Kindly trees in orchards bear
Russet apple, plum and pear;
Leaves turned yellow, gold and brown
From the branches waver down
To the earth from which they came,
Hinting at a lesson I
Have to con before I die:
Death and richness are the same.

THE REVEREND SIMON SIMPLEX FINDS A CRACK IN THE FABRIC

The sky above the church is crowded
With jet-planes and with guardian angels.

Is it the buzz of the former cracks the masonry?
Or the latter's jubilee trumpets as at Jericho?

Mrs Henbane and her coven
Sap the stones with conjurations.

Last night I dreamt I saw
A family of church mice
Vacate the building, all their belongings
Slung over their shoulders in scarlet handkerchiefs:
"We think we could do better on Social Security!"

Lord, one fights on so many fronts.

Holly and ivy brighten up the hall
  To prove that love, like them, is evergreen.
Sign of a gift, proffered to one and all,
Holly and ivy brighten up the hall:
Of berries red as blood, of bitter gall,
  The carol also speaks — with leafy sheen,
Holly and ivy brighten up the hall
  To prove that love, like them, is evergreen.

The Yeti

for Odette Tchernine

Chionanthropus abominabilis (so we'll term him)
Trudged across the Himalayan snows.
From that great height he saw
The Wall of China, the Siberian gulags;
American satellites chirped in the sky above;
He glimpsed the Afghan peaks and sniffed
Spilled oil on the Persian Gulf.
Everywhere man oppressed man, man tortured man,
Man cut man's throat.

"Brother" he grunted "who have called yourself
Sapient, and me abominable —
Your sapience is the knowledge of good and evil.
My breakfast and my lunch are mountain lichen,
Or sometimes I can catch a calling-hare;
But never took a bite out of that apple.

"Well, when you have torn yourselves apart,
And split the world in two, we will be standing,
Ready to take over — and at the door of history, there waits
Another Eden, the same poison-tree."

61

The Corira

Tripping in troops along the Italian shore,
Bold black and white with chestnut,
Curved bill, long legs, toes partly webbed —
Thus the corira, so said Aldrovandus
Four centuries ago. But since his day
No one has found plume or pinion
Or beak or claw of it.

Gryphon, phoenix and simurgh
Flap great mythical wings
Among the heavens of poetry. Plausible corira,
I'll grant you a small place within those realms
Who have this disadvantage — you were not fabulous
But merely non-existent.

The True History of Little Miss Muffet

Little Miss Mouffet was they say the daughter
Of Dr Mouffet, entomologist
And Author of that very learned book
Theatrum Insectarum, and she sat
Upon a tuffet (some texts read "a buffet")
Consuming, with a horn spoon and with relish,
A plain Elizabethan breakfast, curds —
Soft, creamy broken curds, and clear, sharp whey.

The harmony of this idyll was soon shattered.
Came the enormous spider, without a by-your-leave —
Plonked itself beside her, full of menace.
The monster had escaped, without a doubt,
From her papa's vivarium. He often went
On spider forays to get specimens.
But this was no domestic dusty aran,
Who takes hold with her hands, says Solomon,
And gets into the palaces of kings,
Vexation to the Queen and the Queen's housemaids,
Nor garden spinner, cross-emblazoned, throned,
At centre of her geometric web,
Waiting for bluebottles and moths and chafers,
Nor water spider, bringing silver bubbles
Down to the depths, replenishing with air
Her silken and subaqueous bell-tent, nor wolf spider
Speeding over the hard-baked earth, to harry
The quietly munching flocks of caterpillars.
This was a prodigy of the new-found world:
It was Sir Walter Raleigh brought it back
After his Darien voyage, a little gift —
A token of esteem for Dr Mouffet.

It had a grossly swollen hairy body,
Likewise eight twitching hairy legs, and fangs
Ready to plunge themselves into the breast
Of a bright humming-bird, and suck its juices.
The eightfold circlet of its baleful eyes
Seemed always watching her. She screamed, and dashed
Her bowl of curds down to the ground. She rushed
Across the open fields, and then she ran
Slap into the strong arms of a man.

She knew him by his sunburned sailor's mien,
The Spanish cut of his beard, his velvet cloak,
His silver sword hilt, the soft leather pouch
Suspended from his belt to hold his pipe
And his tobacco. Who then should it be
But sweet Sir Walter in his very person.

"My cruddle-cream darling, little whey-faced beauty,"
Thus he coaxed her and he comforted.
In his soft Devon speech "Are you scared of monsters?
You will not find that I am one of those.
I'll take you to the land of El Dorado.
Though there are wild men there, and huge thick serpents
That rear their shameless heads out of the bush,
Nothing shall harm you. You will make them tame —
A virgin captivates the unicorn."

With that he laid her very gently down
Among the buttercups and the moon-daisies.
They lay in the tickling cocksfoot grass, and he whirled her
Round and round the world and back again.

Theatre of Insects

RHINOCEROS BEETLE

This huge scarab, almost
At the limit of insects' allotted size
(Making our country stag beetle a dwarf)
Whose baroque horns and hooks
Suggest rhinoceros or triceratops,
Is bred from a gross grub, ravaging
The luscious cabbage of a palm.

There is a small pinkish toad
That haunts about the houses, puncturing
The enwombing African night
With bell-like, fluting peeps and pings.

A toad and a beetle met in confrontation
Are both scared rigid. The toad observes
A beetle more than twice as big as he is;
The beetle's ganglia obscurely recollect
Toads are cruel murderers of beetles.
Cowards, both of them.

SOLDIER BEETLES

Their worlds the umbels of the wild carrot
Poised high in air, swayed by the summer breeze,
A hemisphere of white flowers, with one
Bright crimson at the centre.

In spite of their scarlet bodies and khaki surtouts
There's nothing aggressive or military
About them. They stray like gentle cattle
And, pig-a-back, they placidly make love.

Eddie Linden, biting into
One of my biscuits, discerned a beestie
Creeping out of a cranny — small and black,
With a trunk like a very miniature elephant;
Two angled and elbowed antennae
On either side of that snout. "Who are you?"
"Who is Eddie Linden?" replied
The coleopteron, "that is the problem.
I am Curculio, the biscuit weevil —
And particularly fond of Bath Olivers.
Mysterious providence, I sometimes think, designed them
Especially for me and my kind.
Eat me, and I am additional protein.
In times gone by, the British sailor
Was all too grateful for that.
I do not question my identity."

LADYBIRD

Ladybird, ladybird, fly away home:
Not yours, but our house is on fire.

We fear the fire from heaven, we fear
Death in the nucleus.

Fly far, small bright beetle, fly far —
Bishop Burnaby, in your scarlet cope —

Fly back to the place of our lost innocence,
The buttercup-fields, the hawthorn-shaded lanes.

A LADYBIRD AMONG THE REFERENCE BOOKS
for Peter Thornber

A two-spot ladybird has elected to hibernate
Between the pages of the *Dictionary of Surnames*,
Among the C's, specifically the Ch's:—
With Chatterton, and Chalmers and Charteris and Charrington.
Sleep snug, Madonnina Coccinella, dry as dust, and secure, we
    hope
From fahrenheit 451. No doomed poet
Shall haunt your winter dreams, but squires and shires
And prosperous brewers — with Lady Chatterley
Going down to the rose-garden with her secateurs.
A plethora of green-fly is upon her roses
All for your delicate feasting.

TIGER BEETLE

Green and gold striped, with elegant
Spiny legs, and cruel slashing jaws,
In an aura of attar of roses,
He runs, with ruthless speed
Seeking his prey, across the vast savannah
That lies there at your feet.

EARWIG

Maligned, the earwig. Unlikely he'd take shelter
Within the labyrinth of your ear, still more improbable
He'd penetrate the brain and start to eat it.
He's safer refuges — dry hedgerow kexes
More appetising fare than that grey soggy blob
Inside your skull, that's stuffed with indigestible
And useless information. He'll devour
The pink and overblown hearts of dahlias,
The golden mop-heads of chrysanthemums,
And the last roses that the summer leaves.

CICADA

A single tettix in a carob-tree
Rooted in dry soil, beside a stony track,
Would almost seem to apprehend our passing
And to resent it too.
He scolds, scolds, scolds, scolds, scolds,
Whirring like a passionate machine —
Drinker of sugary juices, centred in his own world
Of leaves and boughs and long dependent pods
Pregnant with cellulose and butterscotch.

CABBAGE WHITE

The chrysalis split. "It's Spring!" said the butterfly,
Opening to the air in his bridal outfit.
"I'm off — haste to the wedding! — and to tipple nectar;
And no more cabbage, thank you very much."

"Snap!" said the swallow, as he caught him.
"One's always grateful for a snack."

MOTH

The Papal pallium, woven
Of wool from Agnes' whitest lambs;

The heavy, ceremonial mantles,
Commenoi wore, and Palaiologoi;

The partly-tied cravats
Brummel dismissed with a gesture,

Bidding his servant take them to the dustbin
("These, sir, are some of our failures.");

The bridal sheets, smelling of wild woodruff,
Juliet had laid upon her bed —

I've had them all for breakfast, tea and dinner:
A wriggling worm, a small grey moth

That enters, phantom-like, your lamplit room:
I am Time's courier, bearing to one and all

This message: "Moth and rust,
Moth and rust, moth and rust consume".

A HUMBLE BEE

A fumbling, a red-arsed, bumbling bee
Thrust out her tongue into recesses of sweetness,
The florets which composed
A purple clover-head; then flew away
Back to her own untidy nest,
Where wax was mixed with moss, and three queens shared
With a knot of drones, and a dozen or so
Odalisque workers like herself —

"Not so much a hive as a hippy colony," opined
A honey-bee, making a bee-line
To upland moors, and heather honey.

"Thank Buzz some of us have standards.
Long live our socialist hive. We work
For a rational, generative queen." But she was mistaken:
She worked, in fact, for the bee-keeper.

WASPS

The sexless workers, in their tigerish uniforms,
Range, through the balmy days of summer,
With menacing whine and zig-zag flight,
Seizing caterpillars, spiders, flies,
Sawing gobbets from butchers' joints,
To appease the exorbitant larvae,
Snug in their paper citadel.

But summer closes. Death's
In the golden air of harvest. Now they rush
In desperate carouse
On windfall pears and apples, bursting plums
Exuding vinous juices, breathing forth
Intoxicating fumes.

The cold air comes and numbs. For these
No hive's security, no garnered honey stores.

CRANE-FLY

Ineffectual Daddy-longlegs
Dithers and dawdles across the field,
Trailing brittle threadlike limbs;
His body slung between them like a hammock,
He settles on green leaves, among whose roots,
In seasons closed from daylight, he,
A thick tough leatherjacket,
Voracious and esurient, used to gnaw.

FLEA

Hop o'my, skip o'my pollex, Pulex —
    Had I your thews and thighs
I would jump over the dome of Saint Paul's
    To the Dean and Chapter's surprise.

Aphanipteron, siphonapteron —
    If I had got your scope
I would jump over Saint Peter's at Rome
    And show my heels to the Pope.

SILVER FISH

This small survivor, clad in shining scales,
Most primitive of insects has seen them come and go —
Devonian seas, and carboniferous swamps,
The dinosaurs lording it through the secondary epoch,
Then sabre-tooth and megatherium.

It haunts our kitchens now, hiding in crannies,
Through hours of daylight — fire-brat,
It likes proximity of the oven;
When darkness comes, in skipping carnival,
Feeding on scraps, spilt grains of flour and sugar,
The crumbs that fall from the master's table:
For the time being, the master.

The Frog's Return

The frog came back — I mean that one, of course,
Who would go wooing (he was not Monsieur,
The French king's brother, the Duke of Alençon, though
Gloriana nicknamed him her frog, and he too had an unsuccessful
    courtship;
And he was not a brekkek-koaxing aristophanic marsh-frog,
But a fenland nightingale, a yellowbelly,
An honest English *Rana temporaria*,
And kin to Mr Jeremy Fisher.)

This frog, I say, having evaded
Upon the lake the lilywhite duck — or was it a swimming snake? —
Returned, and landed with a loud splash of relief
Back in his native frog pond.

At the sound of that splash, the little blob-black tadpoles,
His nephews and nieces and cousins of every degree,
Like a swarm of errant punctuation marks,
Gathered around to greet the returning hero,
Who'd ventured into such unguessed-at regions —
The world of the amniotic, of the hot-blooded,
Where the mud becomes caked dust, and where
The air under a merciless sun is deathly dry and parching.
They had heard how he set forth to woo
Sweet Mistress Mouse, amid the clatter and bang
Of the flourmill, where light flakes of meal swirled;
Of her Uncle Rat, grisly and yellow-fanged, and the intervention
Of that nine-lived, retractile-taloned monster, Gib, the enormous,
    menacing tabby cat.
"But as for that," said Anthony Rowley (for this, you recall, was
    his name)
"Do not suppose it was any failure of nerve
That sent me scudding back to my native pool.
For have we not braved the pike that lurks in the depths,
The otter, the slinky mink, and the mallard,
Pochard and shoveller — ducks of every description,

And the stream's old grey fisherman, the stalking heron?
It would take more than a cat to make me skedaddle.
Oh no — my resolve to return to the fragrant boglands
Was the fruit of considered and rational reflection.

The whole expedition had been a mistake from the start.
That un-wet world is no place for a frog, and its vaunted glories
Are plainly no more than a load of gammon and spinach.
And as for Miss Mouse, that silken and fabled beauty —
I have to be perfectly frank about this — I viewed her
Not with romantic desire, indeed with repulsion."
"And is it true," chorused the tadpoles, "she's covered from head
        to foot
In fur, she's got whiskers, and ears that stick out from her head,
Paws without any webs, and a long whisking tail?"
"It's true enough," he replied, "but as for her tail,
That in itself should not be looked on with prejudice.
Our cousins, the newts, a most respectable crowd,
They have got tails, you know, and they frequently dine with us.
But there are things that are worse — much worse than the fur,
Than the whiskers, the claws, and the hot, thick blood.
Little ones, you are young, you have innocent souls, and I will not
Spell out for your ears the revolting physiology —
Mammalian coition, parturition,
Lactation, menstruation — but take it from me,
They are foul, those creatures, and the foulest of all is Man —
Though, at first blush, he seems to be almost froglike:
Long-armed, tailless, loud-voiced, nearly naked,
And able to swim — well, after a fashion.
And as for that other warm-blooded kind, the feathered tribes —
I ask you, is there anything more absurd than a bird,
Flopping and flapping about in the yielding air
For all the world as if it were water? And their voices, too,
The ridiculous whistling, screeching fibulation —
That's their idea of music, believe it or not.

"Aeons and aeons ago, in the Carboniferous epoch,
Our ancestors emerged from the primal waters.

They grew pentadactylous hands, and learned to live as adults,
Up in the ambient air — a truly breathtaking achievement,
Which you, little tadpoles, will shortly recapitulate.
We rightly look down on those stupid fish, who could not take
    that step,
Who are tied to a single element — but, to go further,
Would clearly be wrong, would be hubris. So do not stray too far
From your good cool mother, from the womb that cradled you
    when you were spawn,
And lift your thankful hymns to the great Bull Frog —
The Bull Frog in the Sky Whose croak is the thunder,
Whose hop is the leap of the blue-flashed lightning
Springing from raincloud to raincloud — that He, in His providence,
Has placed you here in this pool, in amphibious equilibrium."

Written for a Dinner of the Omar Khayyam Society

There is a tavern in Elysium,
Arboured in amaranth and roses, where
Super-celestial, like a great gold sun,
The wine bowl circulates. And there indeed,
Guests are star-scattered — for Anacreon,
Li-Po, and Horace, and our own rare Ben,
Bellman and Burns are of the company;
Hafiz and Omar have their honoured seats.
There, hiccup never comes nor hangover;
Talk's all good sense and wit, and no-wise slurred,
Nor blurred, nor boring, still less is it tainted
With backbiting or petulance. Tonight
We move into the shadow of that dream.

The Pearl

In my 'forties days, of Soho and Fitzrovia,
The Bricklayers' Arms, affectionately known
To all its regulars as the Burglars' Rest,
Could serve a decent plate of fishcakes, or of shellfish.
I found a pearl in a mussel once
And showed it to the barman. He dropped it on the floor,
And being no bigger than a small pin's head
It was quite irrecoverable. This kind of thing
Tends to occur with all the pearls I get.

Poem to be Written on a Cheque, for Charity

"Money is the life-blood of the poor,"
　　Said Bloy — but the love of it roots for evil:
When Lazarus starves at Dives' door
　　The rich man's sores are licked by the devil.

After Sappho

A fine sight, some say, is a great army
　　Upon the march, or a ship that sails on its way:
But finer the sight of the face that the heart longs for —
　　That is what I say.

Prison Poem

(*from Paul Verlaine*)

The sky is up above the roofs,
    So blue, so calm;
A tree there, up above the roofs,
    Rocks its green palm.

A patch of sky's discerned — a bell
    How gently rings;
Somewhere in that sky, a bird
    Complaining sings.

Dear God — simple and quiet there
    How life goes on!
That peaceable murmur there
    Comes from the town.

What have you done, you here, who shed
    Unceasing tears?
Say, what have you done, and made
    Of your young years?

Autumnal

"We're holed up now," said the bat
In the hollow tree, the hedgehog,
A ball rolled in the leaf-mould,
The earwig in the kex.

"Tartness of rowanberries
I share with my brother scald."
Said the song thrush to the redwing.

"Who feeds us now?" said the Dead,
Ticket-of-leave out of Purgatory,
Glad of a few ungathered bramble-fruits.

"Gold curtains of mist and bronze
Carpets of strewn leaves,
Perfume of regret and trees
Black against white like sharps and flats —
These decorate my salon." said
The gentle ghost of Cecile Chaminade.

Snow

i.

There are three sisters, three grey sisters —
Winter, Old Age and Death. They share
The same keen tooth, they have in common
The same outstaring eye.

ii.

We live between an ice age and an ice age —
A wink of history,
Hunters pursue the mammoth and the reindeer,
Skirting the unretreating ice-sheet. One year,
The snow will come, drift upon candied drift,
And will not go away. The horns of spring,
The trumpets of the summer sound in vain. And then
The Age of Ice resumes.

Moon-Spell

A new moon, God bless her!
Turn the coins in your pocket,
Cupro-nickel — the moon knows
The hidden veins of silver,
Tugs at the secret waters.
Horns of the crescent moon
Be horns of increase.

A full moon, God prosper us!
Turn the apples in the loft.
Magnified by the lens of humidity,
Roundness of the harvest moon be fullness
Of barn and oast house.

A waning moon, God's valediction
On her, on us —
Moon, violated by space shots.
Turn the clods in the field.
Dust in the Council cemetery.
The wheel likewise turns
To cold, to darkness, and renewal.

The Lion and the Unicorn

In Westminster I saw a lion standing —
Parliament, the Abbey, provided the backdrop.
Terribly noble he looked, and terribly sad,
Like a piece of music by Elgar.

A unicorn came wandering
Out of the Caledonian wood. He did not exist,
But his flanks glimmered with moonlight.

The people did not welcome
These additions to their urban fauna.
Some gave them white bread (crumbs
From office sandwiches) some, opining
They needed vitamins, proffered brown,
And some plum cake from media canteens —
Then prepared to drum them out.

"But we will not go", said the beasts, "We are compelled
To support the scutcheon of the British establishment,
Until, approximately, the end of time.
Of course we would much rather return
To our autochthonous habitat —
Sun-beat savannahs, mountains of the moon."

A Genethlion

(for Prince William of Wales, June 21st 1982)

In mournful Paddington the western trains
Clatter and groan. A cry —
It is new life. With our first breath
We take into ourselves the pain of history.

And yet rejoice, rejoice. The month is June —
It's June that brings the red and royal rose,
With cherry-time and strawberry-time. Today I notice
(How London air grows cleaner!) near my window
Martins have built their nest.
With shrill, sharp calls,
With flickering steel-blue wings they
Dart and swoop
Over the roof-tiles and the chimney-stacks.

To Whom It May Concern

(CC, on his 65th birthday)

Missing: the English Muse. Age:
A thousand years and upwards by centuries (but does not look it)
Height: most divinely tall. Colour of hair:
Variously described — hyacinthine, ripe corngold, red
As the red tail of the king of the squirrels. Eyes:
Said to resemble deep woodland pools,
Reflecting broken rainbows, starlight and
Your own countenance undistorted.

Dress: old but serviceable singing robes,
But she has been known to walk down Kensington High Street
Wearing only a laurel wreath (or, alternatively, a coral reef).
Generally carries a carved antique lyre
(Lute, harp, sackbut, psaltery, dulcimer).
Signs of mental disturbance — deceptive:
She is entirely lucid all of the time.

Anyone giving information of her whereabouts
Will be rewarded, but you are warned
There are several impostors around assuming her identity
Messages to her sorrowful and anxious relatives:
Gog and Magog, the Long Man of Wilmington,
Meg and her daughters, the Cerne Giant.

Later — this notice, which has been posted up
In all discos, church porches, natural history museums,
Young ladies' seminaries, opium dens,
And similar places of general resort
Is apparently based on panic, false reporting.
Miss Muse was last sighted crossing the Tamar,
And is stated to be residing with Mr Causley
At number two Cyprus Well,
His address in Launceston.

For George Barker at Seventy

We met on VJ night. Supposedly
Celebrating victory. The cloud over Hiroshima
Cast turbid reflections in the beer.
We have lived in that shadow ever since.

The years pass. The time-gap between us
Somehow furnishes the illusion
That it gets less. The pedantic youth you took in hand,
Slashing pomposities, is now grown into —
Hardly Achilles, but a running man,
Who's always about to catch you by the tail.
He doesn't succeed. And I will call you
A phoenix, not a tortoise.

The Moira extend your thread. Continue,
George, to instruct and delight
Exasperate, excruciate. In the centre of each poem,
Among the smoking cinders, lies
A new-hatched Dionysian deity, imprudently
Wobbling his thyrsus.

Meanwhile, the world grinds on,
Grudging, indifferent. I see you lift
(My God, a dog) a sinister leg against
The off-side rear wheel of Juggernaut.

For David Gascoyne

Enter the whirlpool of the fractured images,
Of the deranged senses — descend
Beyond the images into the darkness,
Climbing down its hairy flanks.
In the depth of the darkness, small but persistent,
A glow. It is the sacred hearth.

The voices, the voices — accusing, denouncing,
Mouthing obscenities, nattering and chattering,
They die into the silence: the absolute silence,
Not of the desert, nor the antarctic waste,
Nor empty spaces between the stars.
In the heart of the silence, the unspoken word,
Its name is Love — the Christ
Of revolution and of poetry.

In Memory of Fr. Geoffrey Curtis C.R.

He brought me his blessing, and he brought a rose.
The rose diffused its scent. I lay
In a hospital bed. The darkness
Slowly encroaching through the years,
Had finally overcome, leaving me free
To recreate the world, from fingertips,
From voices overheard, from images
Vividly remembered, from drifts of scent.
"A gift," said Borges "and it must be used
Like any other gift."
The rose was from the garden of the Royal Foundation.
Matilda, Stephen's wife, had set it up:
And now at Stepney, once a puddly village,
An·island reached by stepping-stones among the marshes;
Exhausted, waiting re-development,
Waiting re-creation. The rose was the blessing.
The Foundation was an act of faith, made in a time
When men built castles, filling them with devils, and it was said,
Openly, God and his hallows slept.

The rose glows in the darkness. In Paradise
Dante saw another Matilda
Gathering the multicoloured flowers.
Katherine also, and Dorothy pluck those blooms — such blossoms
Diocletian's gardens never grew.

Epitaph for Julian Kollerstrom, Mathematician

Number he loved. He was too much alone,
Living in time. And now beneath this stone
His body lies. Trust that his soul may be
Where numbers pass into infinity.

Inscription for a Scented Garden for the Blind

Wayfarer, pause. Although you may not see,
Earth's bright children, herbs and flowers, are here:
It is their small essential souls that greet you,
Mounted upon the morning or evening air:
While from above, from sky and tree-bough,
Birds fling down their songs, a musical burgeoning.

A Little Zodiac

On March uplands the Ram bleats;
    The Bull snorts in the April showers;
Maytime is here, and the youthful Twins
    Are dancing among the meadow flowers.

June, and the Crab and the sun walk backwards;
    The Lion roars the July heat;
In the fruitful fields of August
    The Maiden is gleaning through the wheat.

September — the Balance poises the equinox;
    Scorpion gives an Octoberly nip;
November's centaur Archer bends
    His bow, and lets an arrow slip.

December comes, and the Goat prances;
    The Waterman pours his waters away
In January; in the filled dyke
    Of February the Fishes play.

As the sun moves from sign to sign:
Each upon you sweetly shine.

Two Fishes

For Joanne on her birthday 21 March 1984

Two fishes came swimming up out of February
     Towards the Ides of March,
And one was a dace, or a vendace, or a dory,
     And one was a pollock or a perch.
Snorted the old ram of the equinox:
     "The twenty first bars your way."
"We're going only as far as the twelfth —
     The date of Joanne's birthday."
"How many summers?" "Oh that would be telling!
     But she will be young forever —
The girl who's reading *La Dame aux Camelias*
     Down by the Red River."

Halcyons

Blue flash, darting Alcedo,
Hovering, black and white Ceryle —
Not floating, as the fable told,
In nests of twisted coral on charmed waves;
But long, retreating tides have spared
Their small tunnels on the sandbanked shore.
December, calm of midwinter seas —
The Prince of Peace is born.
Be yours, at turning of the year,
Such halcyon stillness.

The Wise Men of Gotham

The nine wise men of Gotham, thinking
They could detain the spring for ever, built
A hedge around the cuckoo. But, with a twitch
Of his sparrow-hawk wings, and a kick
Of his zygodactylous heels, he's off
Above the holly hedge, and up and away —
Over the sea to Spain.
"You can't hold me!" said he.

Only Joseph's cuckoo-in-the-nest,
Brooded in manger-straw, ensures
Our everlasting spring — the season
Of crucifixion and of resurrection,
Daffodil, crown of hawthorn, cuckoo-flower.

Bird Carol

"Christ is born."
Sang the robin on the thorn.
"Word made flesh."
The wren in the bush.
"In Bethlehem
Is the Sidi Meriem
And the Child she brought forth."
So, at this birth,
The birds of the air
Augmented the choir
Of the cherubim:
"Gloria in excelsis;
Upon the earth, peace," —
Both are one in that hymn.

"That all the World should be Enrolled"

"And there went forth a decree from Caesar Augustus. . ." Some
Have doubted (they were German scholars,
Loathing untidiness) that any government,
For a mere census, could have been so silly,
Forcing everyone to go and seek
The city of his ancestral origin,
Wherever else he might be living now.
For my part, I would cynically opine
That it was just the tomfool sort of thing
Some civil servant would think up, especially
As this was in the Middle East.

                    Well, anyhow,
The roads were all congested, full
Of worried, frightened people, bullied
And badgered by petty officials — rooms
In the hotels booked up, the shops
At profiteering rates, confusion
Of dialects, languages — tongues of the diaspora.
As once across the muddy plain of Shinar
The nations had diffused themselves.

                   In all this messiness
There was one point of stillness — a place
Of cowpats, and of dirty straw, without
Hygiene, and without hot water,
And a beast's feeding trough the improvised cradle,
A space, where back to back,
Covered wagons are parked about a square,
And in that space, a baby's crying — *infans*.

But in that inarticulate cry there breathes
The gemitation of the Dove that brooded
Upon the homeless and chaotic waters; likewise
The rushing of a wind at Pentecost,
And all the bright loquacious dancing flames:
Eternity breaks into history;
The curse of Babel is rescinded.

Two Poems for the Epiphany

i.

"This is your road," sang the bright nova.
"This way, this way!" celestial birds
Shrilled, inside their skulls.

Their paths converged before a gaping cave,
A makeshift shelter for cattle.
The Child — vulnerable, red,
Hairless, with pulsing fontanelle —
Received the unbidden gifts.

Three kings — one, blond and frosty eyed,
Chinked the gold coins; a second, yellow,
Long fingernails sheathed in jade, was grasping
A bundle of joss-sticks; while the third
Black-skinned and curly, offered
The bitter herb that's bred from servitude.

ii.

Winter, a cave, the glittering
Of an unnamed star, to bring
A yellow, a red, and a black king,
With fragrant gum, with gleaming awe,
And with that bitter herb of death:
"Come," said the wind, with icy breath.
"Come, draw near: you touch, you see
The pivot of the galaxy,
The fire that kindles the sun's core —
God's, and man's epiphany."

Before Dawn

for John Cherrington and Bram de Voogdt

I lie awake as I so often do,
In the dead hours preceding morning. If this were London,
In my quiet street there would be silence —
Perhaps the sound of feet, of someone coming
Back from a late party, scraping the pavement,
And then the soft electric hum
Of the early milk-float, until the sparrow begins
To chip away at his one-note song, the collared dove
Reiterating his tedious demotic *dekaokto*.

This is the country. Country is never silent:
Upon the hills the lambs have cried all night,
The ewes replying. With sharp *to-whit to-whit*
A tawny owl quarters her territory;
A mile or so away her rival answers.
In long grass tussocks, woodmouse, bankvole
Scurry for cover, and the young leveret
Crouches in its forme. In the high air
The pipistrelles, with supersonic squeaks
Elaborately dance, pursuing
The pinpoint midges, gnats and moths and beetles.
As the sky whitens, a solitary crow, calling,
Makes a straight line towards the Black Mountains
And now the goldfinch wakes, whose thin twitter
Is like the honeyed scent of the plume-thistle,
Or its soft green prickles; and now the willow-wren
Whose chimes drift down among the fluttering leaves.

They are all here, beyond good and evil —
Redtoothed, blood-clawed — the owl whose brood
Devours each other when rations are short — inviolate,
Although we poison, slash and burn.
We are one step from Eden, and the seraphic blade divides.

And this is Herefordshire. In this golden valley
The red earth's soggy with spilt blood and tears,
The land fought over by the Celt and Saxon
Where every small town has its vigilant castle;
Where Arthur, Offa, and Glendower have trampled,
Now gentle Wye flows on like Gihon. These are the wheatfields,
Orient and immortal, that Traherne
Recalled, that Kilvert looked upon —
As, in their priestly hands, the stuff of time transmutes.